Have a Crumby Book

A COLLECTION OF WIT & WHIMSY FROM CINCINNATI'S FAVORITE BAKERY

NORWOOD
CIRCA 1940s

Have a Crumby Book

BY JOHN ECKBERG

CLERISY PRESS
1700 MADISON ROAD
CINCINNATI, OHIO 45206

Published by Clerisy Press
Printed in the United States
Distributed by Publishers Group West
First edition, first printing

Article excerpts published by permission of the
Cincinnati Enquirer and the *Cincinnati Business Courier*

Library of Congress Control Number: 2007938146

Edited by Jack Heffron
Cover designed by Stephen Sullivan
Interior designed by Laura Moser

Clerisy Press
1700 Madison Road
Cincinnati, Ohio 45206
www.clerisypress.com

Have a Crumby Book

DEDICATION

To Daisie and Joe, who with a sprinkling of flour, a bit of fresh
butter and a handful of sugar created a legacy of sweetness and
delight while taking great pleasure in the baking of it.
-The Busken Family

For Matthew & Rachel
-John Eckberg

CONTENTS

Intro

Drivers don't miss much, even at a mile a minute. That's why interstates throughout Cincinnati and Northern Kentucky are lined with billboards, some lighted in a digital blaze, others old school. Stacked like giant dominoes above a city of homes and businesses, church steeples and cell phone towers, the billboards are seen quickly and often forgotten just as quickly. But the messages of one company rise above the rest and push beyond the realm of advertisement into entertainment, even into a beloved place in our local culture.

The company? Busken Bakery

Busken's messages are funny, clever, and appealing — a blast of whimsy in a churning sea of slogans and signs. Advertising, and particularly the billboard industry, has always been a Wild West corner of American commerce. Promises, pleas, pitches, and hyperbole flash past in a blur. But all went mute when a simple Busken billboard appeared on the cityscape in the summer of 1997.

With bold letters on a white background above the Busken name and the signature bundle of wheat, Busken billboards have become signs of our Cincinnati times. Simple but thoughtful. Wholesome but smart. Like a Valentine's Day cupcake, they're light but filling. They surprise. They delight. They cause us to say to family and friends, "Did you see that? Hilarious."

The standard Busken billboard is usually just a few words. But in the simplicity of a wryly turned phrase or the unexpectedness of a daffy pun, a profound message is whispered to harried and hurrying travelers: enjoy life because life is funny. And while you're at it, treat yourself to a little reward. Buy a Really Happy Face cookie.

The approach has worked well for more than a decade and is likely to keep us smiling for years to come. While we try to avoid most advertising, we look forward to discovering a Busken billboard. We want to see them, much like drivers two generations ago searched for the Burma Shave series of roadside ads.

They represent advertising at its best:

"Have a Crumby Day."

"Your party line starts here."

"You have that glazed look in your eye."

Who can't laugh at the Christmas billboard that turned the sad saga of Rudolph on its head?

"Laugh. Call him names. Eat him."

One Halloween billboard—"Boosken"—violated a fundamental rule of advertising by tinkering with the Busken name and brand. It also carried no sales message whatsoever. Nevertheless, sales exploded.

"Make your milk kinda happy."

"I see hungry people."

"Congratulations are in store."

"Make memories last (at least until dessert)."

The headlines go on and on—as the following pages will soon reveal.

Though the messages are short and simple, the process of creating them can be quite the opposite. Behind each billboard stands a big pile of sketches, scribbles, free-association mumbo-jumbo and plain old hard work—a legacy of brainstorming by teams of creatives and designers at the Creative Department, an agency in Over-the-Rhine where every billboard in the past decade was born.

Steve Deiters, partner/creative director at the agency, remembers the first campaign for Busken and the desperation that spurred it. In 1997 revenues were down because Busken had lost a key retail account. With those outlets gone, the stakes were high for a new ad campaign. The Creative Department scrambled to come up with an approach that would both boost sales and increase brand recognition for the family-owned bakery. After many hours and many concepts, the directors at the agency put together an impressive list of ideas including one by copywriter Michael Comstock that won the day: "Have a Crumby Day."

The phrase became the first board of an iconic advertising effort that still resonates with customers today.

Once the campaign had launched, the pressure was on to create more and better ads. Comstock was one of the people charged with generating them. Day after day, he worked on the project but never, he recalled a decade later, did it feel like work. He always looked forward to developing ideas for the Busken account, and so did his colleague Dave Fagin, who used "wholesome" and "friendly" as guiding winds to fill his creative sails.

Sometimes they made a game of it. At decision-making time, instead of voting thumbs up or thumbs down on prospective billboards, staff at the Creative Department would tape dozens of concepts to a ten-by-twenty-foot wall and puff blow-gun darts at their favorites. Those darts soon got lost, but Comstock and Fagin found they could use plastic bulletin board pins stabilized with tiny fins of tape and shoot them through straws.

As the campaign evolved season by season, messages took on a glib but still jovial tone:

"We're pretty sure it's National Something Day."

"O' Come Get a Faceful".

"Magna Mmm Laude" for a framed graduation photo cake.

One visual quip appeared on the board around the rink where the Cincinnati Mighty Ducks played hockey: "Playing the Mighty Ducks Hurts." That line was followed by a picture of a glazed donut.

Get it?

Playing the Mighty Ducks Hurts, (Don't It)?

Messages were not exclusive to billboards, although that's where most people remember seeing them. The wordplay soon became part of the store experience. Puns appeared everywhere: transparent door clings, door signs, walls, and window posters. They dangled above counters and cash registers and coffee urns. The bakery would have beamed them onto the sides of buildings if it were possible. Point-of-purchase signage planted notions in consumers' minds: maybe I really do need a dozen of those bear claws.

In *Have a Crumby Book,* you'll find your favorite ads collected in one place, where you can savor and enjoy them rather than watching out for traffic. You'll also get a fascinating glimpse into how these witty messages evolved. And you'll see for the first time ever a number of messages that, while hilarious, never made it onto a billboard. They were rejected —and you'll learn why.

The book is organized by seasons, taking you from the start of the year to the end because that's what Busken billboards have been doing for a long time. In this area, we count on Busken ads—as well as their delicious treats—to enrich our holidays, special occasions, and celebrations. To paraphrase a famous movie about baseball, "Busken marks the time."

When the Bengals head to the Super Bowl, Busken billboards commemorate the journey. When Forest Park is in a Mardi Gras mood, Busken and the rest of Cincinnati celebrate with a King Cake billboard that suggests it's time for a new "Louisiana Purchase." When spring arrives in Oakley, Busken billboards arrive with an image of a plate of tea cookies and a funny little plea: "Bring Some home to your peeps." No Halloween in Mack or Montgomery is complete without a billboard of a platter of pumpkin face cookies and the tagline "Made from All Supernatural Ingredients." One year at Christmas, thanks to a Busken billboard in Norwood dedicated to fruitcake, Cincinnatians far and wide realized that this notorious seasonal treat is pretty good after all.

Revisit some of those billboards now within these pages. Chuckle, and maybe cringe, at a wayward pun or two. Laugh out loud if you must. It's true that our time here on earth is short, but it's long enough to enjoy a cookie or two, and it's long enough to laugh at a billboard in the distance.

Next page: Founder Clem Busken and Family Oklahoma City, Oklahoma CIRCA 1920s

BUSKEN BAKERY

Bake all night, sell all day.

Clem & his Wife Amelia

Clem's Children:
Wilbur, Joseph, Margarite Busken

One man,
One dream,
One back-room bakery

Joseph C. Busken Sr. never much liked working in a bakery. He knew how to do it; his father, Clem Busken, had taught him and taught him well at the little bakery back in Oklahoma City. But the hours! The heat! The stress of making products that may or may not sell! Joseph wanted out, though it would be decades—a lifetime, in fact—before that happened. Clem had left Cincinnati for Oklahoma to sell Fleischmann's Yeast, but sales had its own challenges, so Clem turned to the bakery business when he found that a bakery on his yeast route was for sale.

Clem knew little about baking, but since the previous owner was willing to train him, why not make a go of it? The whole family worked in the bakery, including the kids, but his young son Joseph never really warmed to the idea. For one thing, Clem was hard on them, a taskmaster, and the hours were lousy then, just as they are now. Bread and breakfast sweets must be fresh, so they are baked in the middle of the night to be warm and ready for the customers who arrive with the sunrise. A baker in turn-of-the-century America could make a living, but getting rich when profits were measured in pennies and work by the sweat of a 350 degree oven on a hot August night . . . well, Rockefeller luxury was an egg-white mirage.

By the time Joe became a young man, he'd had enough of the dusty flour, greasy shortening, and cloying aroma of fresh-rising bread to last a lifetime. After marrying his sweetheart, Daisie, he packed up his belongings, bid his parents good-bye, and returned to Cincinnati to carve his own path through the world, a path he hoped would have nothing to do with baking. A relative owned a cigar box factory and offered Joe a job. But the company went under, and Joe was now a young man in the town of his

Clem Busken on his yeast delivery route

youth with few close friends, and the Roaring Twenties were about to roar him under.

But he still knew how to bake, knew that he could turn butter, sugar, and flour into nickels, dimes, and quarters, so he approached a small grocer in East Hyde Park with a plan. Why not a bakery in the back room? Joe borrowed five hundred dollars—a small fortune at the time—from the relative with the failed cigar box company, put an oven in the back of the store, and began to sell bread, breakfast sweets, and cookies. He may not have loved baking, but he knew how to do it well, as Cincinnati would soon find out.

Busken's current headquarters was a Ford dealership in Hyde Park in the 1930s

1907

Daisie & Joe Sr. as children

Like all retail bakers, Joe had a tried and true formula. Bake all night, sell all day. And because you can't warehouse donuts and pastries, production must match demand or else Joe and his growing family would eat what they did not sell. Son Joe Jr. was his father's shadow as the bakery grew in output and popularity in the 1930s and 1940s. As a boy, he would go to bed early on Friday nights because the Saturday work alarm would go off at two in the morning, and work followed soon thereafter. As

the 1930s turned into the 1940s and finally into the booming post-war years of the 1950s, Busken Bakery grew at every turn. The storefront in East Hyde Park was gone by now. Locations in Norwood came and went as the Busken empire grew ever larger.

Joe Jr. joined the company in 1952 and through his hard work and creativity the family enterprise expanded. Finally, it became clear to Joe Sr. that his little bakery with its fifty or more employees needed a permanent home, one large enough to supply baked goods for more than a dozen satellite locations.

In 1962, Joe Busken Sr. had to get the biggest loan he could find to pull off what he had in mind. The bakery had run out of space in Norwood again. So this time he decided to look decades into the future. He would buy a failed grocery store at the corner of Madison and Edwards roads and convert it into the biggest and best bakery anybody in Cincinnati

had ever seen. Sometimes you've gotta borrow money to make money, he figured. So, without even telling his oldest son, Joe mortgaged the family land in Indian Hill and the house on it, too. He put everything on the line this time: four decades of alarm clocks going off at two in the morning; four decades of blistering-hot ovens; four decades of wrist burns from wayward trays; four decades of hurry-up from customers on the go; four decades of dime cream horns, nickel glazed donuts and fifty-cent loaves of cinnamon bread; four decades of working on a dream.

Joe put it all on the line for that hundred-thousand-dollar note. Back when he started, he had borrowed five hundred dollars, and that turned out all right. He knew this loan would work out, too, because men who have his drive also have faith. He also knew as sure as the sun shines in the spring that a bakery that sold coffee, donuts, sweets, and breads and did it twenty-four hours a day, seven days a week, would mint money in the emerging new world of drive-ins, four-lane highways, and suburban sprawl.

Joe Jr., who had earned a degree in chemical engineering, went to work on how best to turn his father's dream bakery into a reality of pans, carts, bowls, mixers, ovens, and cake-decorating areas with a beautiful retail store and café out front. He came up with a design that created a circular workflow pattern: commodities would come in through the back docks to a storage area, and the mixing and processing would occur nearby. The heavy mixing zone would give way to six ovens: from the ovens, baked goods would move into the decorating zone or into walk-in freezers, which could also hold unbaked goods. From there, the goods would head to boxing zones and decorating areas back near the loading docks before being shipped to grocery retailing partners or one of the satellite Busken stores. Though Joe Sr. was a bundle of nerves as the contractors moved through the conversion plans—a hawk hovering over every nickel—eventually the store/bakery opened under a homey Tudor/Swiss chalet sign.

With no advance advertising and little fanfare, his gamble paid off. Maybe it was the third-shift workers at the nearby Milacron plant, the LeBlond factory across the street, or the nearby U.S. Playing Card factory. Maybe it was the folks headed to Ivorydale to the Procter & Gamble soap factory. Maybe it was because of the river of cars headed through Hyde Park from Madeira, Montgomery, and beyond to offices downtown, or maybe it was a little bit of all those things, along with a healthy dose of Cincinnati curiosity fed by really tasty baked goods. Whatever it was, within weeks, one thing became clear: Joe Busken's giant bakery was an immediate and immense success.

Breakfast would provide about half the companies revenues, and here's why: eating a baked item or fried sweet for breakfast is a timeless worldwide ritual. Greeks still eat Loukoumades, a sweet fritter dipped in honey and one of the oldest known fried cakes. Italians eat zeppole, the Danish have aebleskiver and in Israel sufganiyols are on breakfast platters. America's appetite for donuts dates to the front lines of World War I, when doughboys were served fritters and coffee by Salvation Army donut

Joe Sr. & Daisie

girls to greet the dawn and, perhaps, their last day. When surviving soldiers returned to the states, they brought their taste for fried, sweet dough with them. Donut shops popped up everywhere, thanks to automated fryers.

It was a trend destined to stick around and to-day Americans eat more than 20 million donuts daily—more than eight billion donuts a year. Nine of 10 Americans eat donuts with men eating more donuts than women and teenagers the next largest

BUSKEN'S
MARIEMONT SQUARE

BUSKEN'S
MILFORD SHOPPING
CENTER

BUSKEN'S
PLEASANT RIDGE

BUSKEN'S
CHERRY GROVE PLAZA

BUSKEN'S
KENWOOD PLAZA

BUSKEN'S
HYDE PARK SQUARE

A few of the Busken stores back in the day.
CIRCA 1960s

consumer group. Within two generations of those World War I doughboy, donuts were firmly entrenched in America's morning ritual.

In 1970, Page Busken joined his brother, Joe Jr., in leading the company. By then, breakfast sweets and donuts from the bakery in Hyde Park had a 24/7 hold on the lives of most Cincinnatians. The brothers continued to add stores, committed staff to new products and new services, too: corporate catering, fund-raising programs, and corporate gift-giving during the holiday season.

They also recognized that, as more and more women entered the workforce in the 1970s, downtown Cincinnati offered a great opportunity for affordable lunches from a homegrown bakery/restaurant. Busken opened its first combo cafe/bakery at 210 E. Sixth Street in 1977. A second came at Eighth and Walnut in 1980. In the 1980s, a restaurant was added to the Norwood store and yet another bakery/restaurant opened at Ninth and Central Avenue in 1989.

When the Web created new retail opportunities, Page committed the company to nationwide distribution. This time it was click-of-mouse and not word-of-mouth that would bring in customers. Cincinnatians responded, too. For some the Busken Bakery was a convenient and quick stop before church on Sunday mornings. For others, the visit came after church. Weekends, the bakery became a destination for late-night repasts. And as always there were birthdays, anniversaries, retirements, and graduations.

But it takes more than regional food habits and demographic trends for a family-owned food company to survive through generations. Analysts report that only about one in three family businesses in America successfully moves from the first generation to the second generation. Busken Bakery is among the 10 to 15 percent of companies that thrive into the third generation of family ownership and control. One reason for its success has to do with a critical rule for family members who want to become part of the Busken management team: work for at least three years for another company in another field. Named president of Busken in 2007, Daniel, a grandson of company founder Joe, worked in construction. Brian, also a grandson and today the director of marketing, was a copywriter at an advertising agency.

Busken Bakery has always embraced a strategy of growth to remain vibrant, and the newest Busken generation plans to maintain that approach. Daniel and Brian are steeped in the family's bakery tradition. As youngsters, they once ran their own bread and breakfast treat route. Later, they routinely came to the bakery early on Saturday mornings with their father or their grandfather. The birth of Cake Town, group tours of the bakery itself, creating a zone dedicated to birthday parties and celebrations, the introduction of new smoothie-style drinks, and other products like two-cookie packs at convenience stores—all show that the line between entertainment and the bakery craft has blurred.

Anybody who has ever watched a kid watch a donut-frying machine knows that. And anybody who has ever snuck in a bite from a box of still-warm Danish knows it, too. Busken Bakery, with its deep family roots, quality products, and friendly Cincinnati-style service, will remain a Cincinnati institution for decades—if not centuries—to come.

SPRING

Object
of your
Confection

It's always a bonus when you can create a billboard with a built-in jingle. Just try to look at the billboard above and NOT hum Everly Brothers the rest of the day.

Get some.

"What the World Needs Now" popped out just after the riots. We wanted to take the message to the people and allow Busken customers to join in with printed yard signs. It would have worked, too, if not for that crazy little thing called "budget."

What the world needs now.

Busken

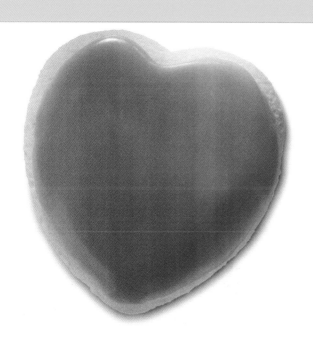

When mini-cookies came out, we had a communication problem: you can't tell relative size with just one cookie on white. So we went to multiples and varied the sizes to give the billboard interest and life. (Of course, it always took eating several tubs of these delicious little morsels to land on the perfect arrangement.) Work. Work. Work.

Your place or ours?

Be fresh anywhere in the world. Visit www.busken.com

Love portion.

Busken

More romantic than a bear claw.

Get a little fresh.

Busken

Ten years of headlines and we can still be fresh on Valentine's Day.

So many concepts. So few billboards. Naturally, we went to t-shirts to get more ideas on the streets—which opened up a whole new frontier—especially for Valentine's Day.

Hey, sweet cakes.

Who Came Up with this Bright Idea?

It seemed like such a good idea at the time: use an image of a cupcake on a billboard. The date for the photo shoot, however, snuck up on the bakery during Christmas week, so very little planning went into the ad, and in the end, with the photographer waiting, a baker came up with a cupcake that was beyond cute. Iced in scarlet, the cupcake also had seven candy hearts arrayed on top. Four thin lines of icing in white and pink swooped along the crown in an intricate pattern. It was a beautiful cupcake— and virtually impossible to produce in mass. It's one thing for a baker to make one intricate cupcake. It's another thing to make seventeen hundred of them in one weekend.

Customers saw the beautiful cupcake on a billboard on the Norwood Lateral, and the orders poured in. Decorators were swamped. They went crazy trying to handle this improbable—no, impossible—challenge. Because the cupcakes that came out of the bakery looked only a little like the one on the billboard, customers were annoyed or disappointed, or both. They let the counter staff know it, too, as Cincinnatians are never shy about expressing displeasure.

Bakery Lesson Number 33,465: never use a cupcake that might win a baking contest on a billboard.

For hearty appetites.

Fill that empty spot inside. Busken

O' the possibilities with St. Patrick's Day. An outdoor board concepting session produced a couple of little gems that could work as fun door clings at all Busken locations (not to mention leprechaundominiums).

O'Goodie.

Busken

"Get lucky" and "You could use a little luck" basically say the same thing. But the former is quicker and richer in meaning—which is why it was fortunate enough to be produced. And the latter, well, just became a footnote.

Sham dunk.

Busken

How much temptation can a person take?

Show us your forks.

Busken

MARDI GRAS KING CAKES ARE HERE

Keep your shirt on.

King Cakes are back. Busken

As wild as it is, Cincinnati is NOT New Orleans. Maybe that's why we opted for the concept on the right instead of the left.

Big. Easy.

Send a King Cake anywhere at busken.com

Busken

Fat Tuesday.

Diet Wednesday.

Busken

Sometimes great concepts require a set-up and a punch line. This two-parter found a home on both sides of a dangler hanging in Busken stores just before Mardi Gras.

Cajun just taste it.

Busken

The King Cake dough is braided. On the "Try something twisted" billboard we're counting on that coming through in the photo.

Try something twisted before Lent.

Busken

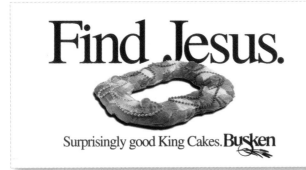

The traditional King Cake has a plastic baby Jesus hidden inside. The one lucky enough to get that special piece with baby on board earns the honor of buying the next cake. Although we couldn't bring ourselves to run "Find Jesus" it does make us smile every year when we pull out the concepts.

Mardi Gras King Cakes.
Bayou one.

Busken

All jell could break loose.

This one was a Toughski for the creative team. The Paczki was a total unknown: an overstuffed jelly-filled Polish donut with a Gordian Knot of a name—once you get past that, it's a pretty awesome product.

Polish one off.

Try a Paczki (Poonch'-key).
The Über Jelly Donut from Poland.

Busken

Yumski.

Try a bite of a Paczki (Poonch'-key), the Über Jelly Donut from Poland. **Busken**

CIRCA 2007

The World's Cutest Chicken Coop

The Great Depression came and went and with it a hundred or so chickens that once upon a time lived behind the Busken family house in Indian Hill. To avoid offending any Indian Hill neighbors, the Buskens built this chicken coop to look like a dollhouse. As long as you could ignore the dozens of chickens pecking in the dirt in the fenced area outside, it was probably the nicest-looking coop in the history of egg production: a full-sized door, working windows, window frames, shutters, cedar shake siding, and, above the little doors where the chickens came and went, a nice bit of trim.

Bakery products, as the Starbucks coffee chain would discover decades later, can be profitable. Bakeries convert items purchased at commodity prices into affordable luxuries, essentially turning pennies into dimes. The easiest raw material for a baker to get is an egg, as long as the dedicated baker has a kid who is able and willing to collect the eggs each morning and feed the chickens each evening. During the Great Depression, when jobs in Cincinnati disappeared at a staggering rate, the eggs for the Busken frosting, meringue, and about a hundred other items came from this quaint little chicken house.

Eventually, as Joe Jr. grew from child to man, managing more than a hundred birds (the coop headcount supposedly topped out at 140) became too much of a chore for a son who was now in college. The solution? Easy enough. Big platters of fried chicken and kettles of steaming chicken and dumplings. One day the chickens and their eggs were gone. But the chicken coop? It's still standing. As a matter of fact, it still looks good, too.

Happy Eater.

Busken

Busken cupcake on eBay

By Chuck Martin
The Cincinnati Enquirer

It must be the highest-priced cupcake in Cincinnati history. And it's certainly the first time the bakery that made the cupcake has bought it back on eBay.

But this is no ordinary cupcake. In 1994, a friend gave Ken Lay of Westwood two Busken Bakery Easter chick cupcakes. He gobbled one, but couldn't eat its twin because it was "too cute."

So he returned the sweet bird to its original box and stuffed it in the freezer.

Now, 10 years later, Lay is about to marry Mary Bryan, who has three young daughters. To make room in his freezer the ancient cupcake has to go. Instead of toss-

ing it, Lay's family put it up for auction last week on eBay. Just for fun.

Little did he know, Busken stopped making the chick cupcakes eight years ago. Maybe it really is a collector's item.

A colleague at Lay's graphic design firm bid $1 – not bad, considering the cupcake originally cost 69 cents. Then a reporter from an Erie, Pa., newspaper called about his unusual item. Next, someone from Busken Bakery phoned to say the company wanted to buy the chick cupcake.

"I told them that if they bid whatever it takes to win it and donate the equivalent in cookies or something to charity, they could have it," Lay says.

Busken's winning bid was $52.51. The company will donate pastries worth that amount to Cincinnati's Children's Hospital Medical Center.

This 10-year-old chick cupcake sold on eBay.com Friday.

A former Busken marketing director refused to let us run the "marshmallow chicks" board, believing the phrase evoked images of overweight women. We knew we were just referring to our Peeps. It ran the year after he left.

Marshmallow chicks dig us.

Busken

Be somebunny.

Rabbit Season.

Duck Season.

"Eat da bunny." You may have to say this one aloud a couple times before you get it. As fun as it is, it never appeared for one simple reason: Busken didn't have a cutter to make bunny cookies. Oh well, maybe next year.

44

Great for your peeps.

Busken

CIRCA 1940s

Baking Is Not Cooking

Never ask a baker how something was cooked. His likely reply? It wasn't cooked at all—it was baked. He might roll his eyes first, though, and frown just a little in impertinent impatience. A baker bakes. Period. (Except when he's, say, frying donuts, but don't ask him about why that isn't cooking, because he is, after all, a baker, and bakers can be moody, so it's better not to ask.) Just remember, bakers don't cook. Never have. Never will.

March sanity.

Busken

SUMMER

One smart cookie.

Straight AAAAhs.

Grad Cookies, Grad Photo Cookies, and Grad Photo Cakes.
We have what you need to face the future
with a smile. Order yours early 871-CAKE. **Busken**

Pride and joy.

Graduation cookies. **Busken**

We had to comb through dozens of cookies for this shot. It was really tough to find a graduation hat that didn't make our Really Happy Cookie look like Paul Revere. Maybe we should sell these on Independence Day too.

Buy a dozen.
(One for each year.)

Graduation cookies. **Busken**

Here's to you, Mrs. Robinson.

We took the grad photo specifically to get that deer-in-the-headlights look. It played perfectly to the "Stick a Fork" headline and then some.

Stick a fork in him. He's done.

Congratulations
are in store.

871-CAKE
(871-2253 for underclassmen)

Busken

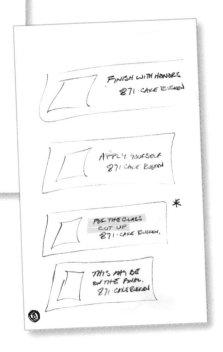

Like a school jacket.
Only moister.

On the next page, it took two photos to pull off the seemingly simple billboard. The grad was taken by Kuchik Photography, our go-to guy for great people shots. The cake was expertly captured by Teri Studios, one of the premiere food shooters in town, who helped us capture our first eight years of Busken deliciousness.

Cram after finals.
Busken

Congratulations

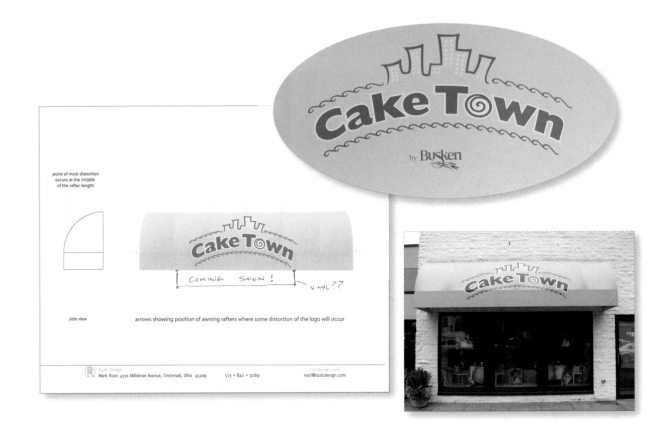

point of most distortion
occurs at the middle
of the rafter length

COMING SOON!

VINYL??

side view

arrows showing position of awning rafters where some distortion of the logo will occur

Rozic Design
Mark Rozic 4310 Millsbrae Avenue, Cincinnati, Ohio 45209   513 • 841 • 9169   rozicdesign.com
mail@rozicdesign.com

The Cakery. Caketorium. Cake Canaveral. We had come up with four pages of names for Cake Town before settling on just the right balance of fun and cakiness.

here, a scroll
broad swash of
on Cami Smith,
she decorates
day cake at
ati headquar-
ecorator is a
operation at
tore and pro-
ted to create a
e for children,
e what goes on
Brian Busken,
th generation of

tinued on page 12)

Kids and Cakes

The strong purple letters and faux skyline on a rich golden canopy above the door at Busken Bakery on Madison Road says it all for any red-blooded kid in Cincinnati. Cake Town. Kids must wonder, "Can it get any better than this?" as they sprint from car to front door. And inside they'll find plenty of wonder, even though Cake Town is just a baker's table anchored by decorator and Cake Town Mayor Cami Smith. Nearby is a bench for small people to sit and watch. Kids flock here to watch Smith bring beauty to a simple yellow layer cake.

Quick squeezes of big and colorful frosting bags soon bring flowers and leaves—or a football field. Layer cakes stacked atop one another become scenes of delight. Cake Town was an experiment to see whether bakery retailing could be entertainment. Within one year of its introduction and with no advertising, cake sales grew by twelve percent. For a homegrown family-owned bakery, that was sweet success.

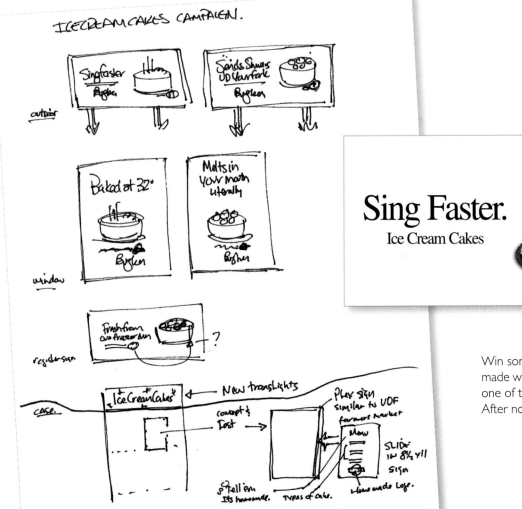

Win some. Lose some. The Busken Ice Cream Cake made with genuine UDF Homemade Ice Cream was one of those brilliant ideas that never really took off. After not even a year, we retired the Freezer Oven.

We're pretty sure it's National Something Day.

Busken

Celebrate with cake.

Open your
cake hole.

Busken

Cut One
Today.

Busken

It's a
pieces of cake

For some strange reason these never ran.

CIRCA 1950s

Let Them Eat Cake

Decorators expect a busy morning in the Busken cake room—aka the Art Department—on this first Saturday in May. The room holds hundreds of cakes in identical trays and aluminum racks, and under each is a work order that will shape the morning for the decorators in this room that is equal parts artist studio and bakery. It's graduation season. People are always celebrating birthdays, retirements, confirmations and reunions. It's also Kentucky Derby day, and dozens of cakes have been ordered for derby parties.

"We sure made some horseshoe cakes yester-day, didn't we," says Krysta Guthrie as she feathers the trigger on an air brush gun that dusts blue skies onto some birthday cakes, green fields onto others. Today, some will spread icing, others will apply script, and some will squeeze icing tubes to create roses, baseball fields, borders, and rich green vines.

Each Saturday, the first thing decorators do is make writing tubes: triangles of parchment paper become cones and then are filled, one by one, with a dozen icing colors. Tips are soon snipped and script and flower stems follow. Some decorators stack cake atop cake, first a small round layer, then a larger round, and finally another small round. Then comes the icing that turns a tipsy tower into a soccer ball. Magic. A Barbie doll emerges from one conical layer cake. Each row of icing looks like lace on a Victorian dress that spills from the doll to the tray below. It is only hours before the party. The centerpiece will be something no little girl would ever forget. Each year these decorators create about 70,000 cakes and that, of course, equals many celebrations. By midmorning nobody speaks. Elsewhere people are mowing lawns, cleaning gutters, doing Saturday chores. Here, decorators quietly create memories.

CIRCA 1959

Susan Busken Hunter as Little Ms. Muffin. Represented the Cincincinnati Retail Bakers Association in this National Competition sponsored by Procter & Gamble.

A Bakery Route of Their Own

It seemed like such a good idea: teach the young grandsons of founder Joe Sr. a bit about sunrises on Saturdays at a bakery, a bit about baking, a bit about logistics of food retailing, and a lot about customer relations with a bakery route of their own.

Christian, Brian, and Dan took to the task with glee as they went knocking on doors on their street in Mount Lookout to take orders for the following Saturday. Cinnamon bread here. A half-dozen donuts there. Danish here. Coffee cake there. Smiles all around. Their father Page woke them at 5 a.m. and tumbled into the VW bus to head down to the bakery.

Filling orders was tougher than it sounds, because these were young boys and writing and arithmetic were skills acquired only a few years before. But they threw themselves into the work, finding each item, wrapping each while still warm. Their red wagon was full when they set out, and for a few weeks everything was fine.

Almost everything. One neighbor complained. She accused the kids of price gouging (didn't happen), and of pocketing the quarter tips (which they did with glee, of course). So the boys' business was shuttered, and store coupons went out to all the neighbors to smooth over any hard feelings.

That service is but a memory now, but for one fine season on one street in Mount Lookout, families had fresh-baked goods delivered to the door. And after each delivery, a happy kid skipped back to his red wagon: happy he had a quarter tip of his own in his pocket and happy that another delivery was only moments away—maybe another quarter tip, too. Change jingled in those boys' pockets as they strutted into summer.

Baked 75 years ago and still pretty good.

Yes, it's our anniversary. So celebrate with a free taste of an original goodie.

To celebrate the 75th anniversary, we broke with tradition (funny enough) and went with a whole retro look featuring our pioneer Joe Busken Sr., but that same great dry wit.

A celebration
75 years in the baking.

Goes great with
chocolate or white milk.

We toyed with the idea of improving race relations in the city with a smile—and quickly ran to the safety of Sixties nostalgia instead.

Flour children.

Busken

One of our very first explorations into the power of the Really Happy Cookie. Could have been quite engaging, but at the time we only had the budget to shoot the cookie part.

Busken

Proud supporter of people who eat.

As eaten on TV.

Our famous iced cookies available for delivery, fundraising and the occasional autograph. Busken.com

Although everyone calls these Smiley Face Cookies, they are officially Really Happy Cookies. Page Busken got a couple of threatening letters from a guy in Pennsylvania who claims to own the rights to the words "Smiley Face" (and is apparently not keen on sharing).

Have a crumby day.

Busken

You No Pay!

Loyalty to Busken knows few boundaries. A billboard with the word "Basken" was placed along the Norwood Lateral in the late—1990s during the dog days of summer. Showcasing a yellow cookie backlit by a blaze of sunny rays, the ad implied that summer fun went hand-in-hand with a Really Happy Face cookie. Then an anxious call came to the Busken offices from an outraged fan.

"I have to tell you, I have to tell you," the man said. He spoke with an Asian accent. "They spelled your name wrong! You no pay. You no pay."

When Page Busken, son of founder Joe Sr., tried to explain that the word was a play on the phrase "Baskin' in the sun," the man would have none of it. "I don't get it," he replied. "I do not understand." And then he returned to his original refrain. Maybe if I repeat it a few more times, the man must have thought, this baker on the other end of the phone line will finally understand.

"You no pay," he insisted, certain of his public service. "You no pay."

Basken

Changing with the times has always been a hallmark of the Busken survival story. Coolies have become a sweet addition to this story.

It's happy hour.

Try one of our delicious Cookie Coolies.

Smooth operators standing by.

Busken Cookie Coolies

Happy Frappe
Smile Face Iced Cookie Frappuccino

	Medium	Large
	2.99	3.75

Classic Mocha Chip
Chocolate Chip Mocha Frappuccino

Coffee Coolies

		Medium	Large
Original Espresso	Iced {	2.49	3.20
Vanilla			
Caramel			
Mocha	Blended {	2.99	3.75
Chai			

Smoothie Coolies 100% cool fruit

	Junior	Medium	Large
Mango			
Strawberry	1.99	2.99	3.75
Strawberry/Banana			
Four Berry			
Green Tea			

Kid Coolies Includes Sprinkles

	Junior	Medium
Frosty Bubble Gum		
Chocolate Marshmallow	1.99	2.75
Orange Cremesicle		
Cotton Candy		

Coolies are only available at the Madison Road Busken—the test market location to see if this concept has "legs."

Iced Coffee Coolies

Cookie Coolies

Kids Coolies

Smoothie Coolies

Try our Cincinnati chilly.

Ask about our Coffee Coolies.

AUTUMN

Fifteen minutes before our first Busken Halloween presentation, Dave Fagin was playing around with a concept that had no headline. Just the classic pumpkin cookie and the Busken logo. Well, not exactly the Busken logo. Not even the Busken name. It just said "Boosken". An inside joke that everyone in Cincinnati would get. We printed it out (making us fifteen minutes late for the meeting). Page Busken laughed. Then decided to let it run— and it paid off in record sales. This idea set us up to take chances on Busken boards from that moment on.

Boosken

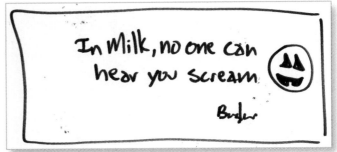

The movies gave us ample opportunity to play. But only rarely did one of these ideas make it to prime time.

I see hungry people

Boo-Dey.

Busken

Now thru last
eek in October.

Send delicious Halloween cookies anywhere in the world at busken.co

The best ones keep the message deceptively simple. There's almost always a deeper meaning
to be found if you look for it.

Frighten your milk.

Boosken

CIRCA 1960s

The Bakery Business Has Its Perks

Nothing is left to chance at Busken Bakery—or any other thriving company, for that matter. At Busken planning meetings, which occur every eight weeks, there is one other unspoken rule: if you leave the room hungry, it's your own fault.

Each meeting begins with—what else?—breakfast treats, snacks, and dinner desserts. They flow to the conference tables in a river of baking sheets, a couple hundred bucks worth of irresistible luxury coming

one after another, chopped into bite-sized pieces that are always tasty and filling. When half of company revenues stem from morning sales—people stopping off for coffee and perhaps a Danish for the road, or maybe two dozen donuts for the company's coffee alley, or a swell cake to celebrate a colleague's birthday—it's no surprise that most of these platters scream breakfast. It's a carnival of consumption: cherry, cheese, and blueberry Danish for the Fourth of

CIRCA 1960s

July. Cherry strudel glisten next to warm cinnamon streusel crumb cake. Wonderful slices of blueberry cake (with a hint of buttery rum ... or is that a whisper of lemon?) materialize alongside lemon crumb cake and blueberry/cream cheese Danish.

Questions cascade from the Busken team and the reps from Northern Kentucky-based Remke Markets, retail partners who are here to plan upcoming seasonal events.

Together they try to figure out what customers want, what they need, and what will surprise them. When are the red-white-and-blue tea cookies going to arrive? Customers are asking for them. Can cupcakes have a scene from the movie Cars on top? Would customers buy individual strawberry pies, or will the crust of a three-inch-diameter pie overwhelm the fruit? Is it time for another parking-lot festival? Will peach bits satisfy a peach muffin buyer? Should twelve Danish on a boxable tray include four varieties or three? Back to the parking-lot festival: will cupcakes melt in the heat?

On and on the questions come, as morning lurches toward lunch. Nobody in this room will be hungry anytime soon.

Coffee with whipped scream.

Kicker treat.

Come in for Coffee Busken

Eventually we began extending the Halloween offering beyond pumpkin cookies, and people ate it up.

Let your little monsters feed.

Creative Party Cakes they'll howl about. **Busken**

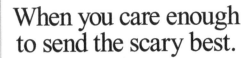

When you care enough
to send the scary best.

Treat friends anywhere in the world to bakery-fresh cookies: www.busken.com

Gourdgeous

Busken

August is when we do most of the concepting for the Halloween billboard and in-store signs, which generally runs the entire month of October. It usually takes about a week of sleepless nights to produce two or three headlines worthy of posting. It's wicked fun.

They're creepy
and they're cookie.

Boosken

Looks like a case of the Heebie Jeebies.

Fill up your spookie jar.

Halloween cookies delivered frighteningly fast at busken.com **Boosken**

We wanted the mini-cookies for Halloween to have their own identity. By branding them Heebie Jeebies, we created a snack as fun to eat as they are to give someone.

Horror
d'oeuvres.

Boosken

Busken Cookie Poll

May the best cookie win.

WINNING COOKIES: So then, the baby's born, the count is in and the cookies were right. Again.

Referring here to **Jati,** the Cincinnati Zoo and Botanical Garden elephant who delivered a 213 pound boy at 4:50 a.m. Sunday.

Page Busken, recall, did a poll at all stores, wherein customers could buy a blue or pink cookie based on their guess of the baby's gender. Just like its Super Bowl where customers buy cookies to vote on the winning team.

Page Busken

Busken customers went for a boy: 1,614 to 1,600, so the streak continues: Super Bowl polls have been right 11 of 13 times.

Your Party Line Starts Here

Republicans and Democrats do agree on something: a Busken cookie tastes pretty good. After the success of the Busken cookie poll on Cincinnati's favorite football team leading up to Super Bowl XXIII, bakers at Busken decided to turn the tables on voting. In 1992 they made and sold cookies with the faces of Bill Clinton and the elder George Bush on them, and the Busken staff kept close count. The results of the first political cookie poll astonished everybody, as it came within two percentage points of the nationwide ballot-box tally. Future cookie polls in every major election since were equally astute.

Busken Bakery went global one year when NBC's *Today Show* included the results of the cookie poll in a morning broadcast on Election Day. That year those not close to a TV could hear radio commentator Paul Harvey detail how sales of a simple sugar cookie in Cincinnati could predict the voting trend of a nation of 300 million people. Never underestimate the power of a Busken cookie or the votes cast by cookie monsters in Greater Cincinnati to mirror a nation.

Rich & Flaky

Yeah, they're
both soft.

...ential Cookies $1.09 Busken

Follow
your gut.

Presidential Cookies $1.09 Busken

These go back a few years. Kerry. Gore. Bush. Who did you buy at the time?

Political instore.

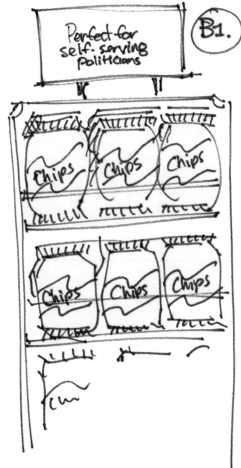

Perfect for self. serving Politicians

B1.

Chips   Chips   Chips

Chips   Chips   Chips

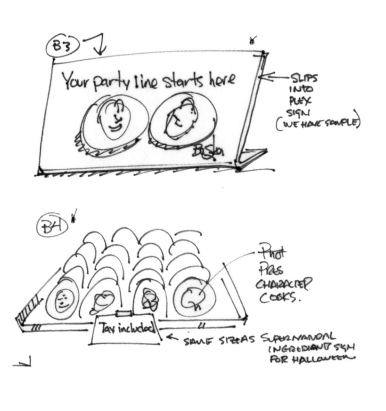

B3

Your party line starts here

SLIPS INTO PLEX SIGN (WE HAVE SAMPLE)

B.Sign

B4

Phot Pres CHARACTER COOKS.

Tax included

SAME SIZE AS SUPERNAND INGREDIENT SIGN FOR HALLOWEEN

The traditional American two-party system gave us more than enough fodder to run with.

Presidential Cookie Poll

Each cookie ordered counts as a vote for your favorite candidate. For the sweetest of victories, we suggest stuffing the ballot box. Often.

Presidential Poll

Support the crumby politician of your choice.

Choose me.

No, me.

Busken

Both parties could save a lot of money if they drop the whole primary process and go to a pure Cookie Poll system. Weirdly enough, this method hasn't failed yet.

Buy an election.

Presidential Cookies $1.09 **Busken**

Eat in or
Kerry out.

And the
loser is...

Daily Busken Poll

Either way
you pay.

No crumb goes
uncounted.

Presidential Cookies $1.⁰⁹ Busken

Please,
no hanging
crumbs.

Presidential Cookies $1.⁰⁹ Busken

PERFECT FOR
SELF-SERVING
POLITICIANS

ORE   BUSH   GORE

Refunds accepted here.

$1.^{25}$ at a time.

CIRCA 1960s

Cream Horn High Jinks

Joe Jr. was four years old when he went down to his dad's bakery in Pleasant Ridge with his mother to watch his father work. Joe Sr. always ready with a quip or a practical joke, put his son on top of four bags of flour near the work counter so father and son were eye to eye. He was filling cream horns with sweetened, whipped egg whites—every child's vision of heaven. The father told the son to open his mouth, and when he did, Joe filled the boy's mouth with a blast of filling. The lad could still breathe, but he couldn't swallow, and he couldn't think about anything other than this: too much of a good thing is probably not a good thing.

"I didn't cry," Joe Jr. remembers. "I didn't swallow. I just stood there. I was so shocked. But I remember it to this day."

You want it.
We knead it.

(Order Thanksgiving rolls and pies by November 16.)

Order forms available in all food service areas.
5% of overall profit to benefit Children's Hospital.

Make sure you're welcome.

Not every idea is a big seller. "Thanks" cookies seemed like the perfect thing to share at Thanksgiving. Although it worked on paper, people still went for the pumpkin pie instead.

Let us give

Thanks

Make sure you're welcome for the holidays.

WINTER

Changing times demand foresight, understanding of the market and generating ideas to appeal to that market.

So dinner rolls have given way to bagels, layer

"Customers need a way to justify buying something with higher fat and sugar content," he said. "Our product represents a celebration, a

---

A billboard Busken used to try to sell more cookies at Christmas backfired. They sold out of fruitcake instead. "A lot of people said, 'Well, I'm last century,'" president Page Busken says.

What a Christmas gift. If only we could have more failures like this one.

Fruitcake is so last century.

Tea Cookies Mean Home

Kay and Jack Cluxton live in far-flung Aberdeen, Ohio, a river town steeped in history and the green hills of southern Ohio and washed by an ancient light found only in hamlets on broad inland rivers. And it's a long way from Aberdeen to the Busken Bakery on Beechmont Avenue in the humming suburban heart of Anderson Township, but that was where the Cluxtons found themselves one morning. They were on a road trip, a monthly jaunt to Lexington, Kentucky, and they were here because they wanted to bring their daughter, her husband, and their Kindergarten grandson a sack of treats: butter tea cookies, each about one and a half inches in diameter, and each topped with a colorful dab of icing.

The Cluxtons knew their daughter had loved these cookies when she was little, explained Kay, a native of Cincinnati's West Side and someone who must still be fairly fond of them herself as she and Jack had just gone fifty miles out of their way to buy some. They were now farther away from Lexington than when they started their journey, and they had another ninety minutes of three-lane interstate highway to go. But they had their Busken cookies. And a family tradition had touched another generation.

Love one. And another.

Busken

Tastes 50% better
than most greeting cards.

Busken

Santa has a card
up his sleeve.

Busken B
GIFT CARD

Okay, we totally made up the taste claim. But we secretly seeded the idea that delivering a small cookie tray is a delightful way of sending a message (and it doesn't leave a crumby of evidence).

This year, send stuffing.

Holiday cookies delivered anywhere in the world: busken.com.

Santa Claus is going to town.

Busken

Eat up. We have
eight maids a milking.

Busken

Headline Schmedline. Adding the "Schm" sound to any word is usually the first concept we generate as a warm-up and the first one we trash. But there was something about Schmelves that made us giggle like schoolgirls. So we kept it.

Elves Schmelves.

Send a holiday assortment anywhere in the world. Just visit www.busken.com

The "Just be Claus" line had it all for us. Double entendre. Quick. Endearing. Call to action. This is the type of headline that keeps on giving.

Economine In 1959

No bakery grows from a single oven in the back of a small grocery into a regional food titan without a ton of effort and a driving passion from dozens of bakers, decorators, clerks, and administrative staff. That level of growth takes years, eventually stretching into decades and, for the lucky few, maybe even centuries. During each era Joe Sr. held true to an unspoken mission: just bake it right, and it will sell.

The names and faces of the men and women who came to work—sometimes in the wee hours of the morning, sometimes in the heat of a Cincinnati August—have faded into time. A few locations are only memories: in Hartwell, in East Hyde Park, on Hyde Park Square, and on Sherman and Williams avenues in Norwood.

It's said that founder Joe Sr. was a fastidious baker. No dusty counters full of wayward flour, no spilled shortening on the floor, no unwashed pans lying all about. What's not as well known was that he was an equally fastidious bookkeeper. A letter written to his daughter, Linda, in January 1959 offers insight into what made him tick: fretting over pennies and nickels. He praised his daughter for improving her grades and then offered an accounting of her college costs down to the penny: "clothes etc., $631.19; insurance, $151.64; cash, $1,500." He already had made a similar list for himself, his wife, Daisie, and son, Page. Each was measured down to the penny.

"You probably wonder why this has not been brought up before," he wrote. " Dollars did not roll in as easy as last year. Taxes are high, and I have a feeling we are not spending our money wisely or that we have spent it too loosely. I went over the whole accounting with Mother and Page and will with you also when we get together. Business has been spotty.

"After going over 1958 accounting, I have adopted the slogan Economine in '59."

Take care of pennies, Joe knew, and nickels will soon emerge and grow into dimes and quarters. The dollars, well, the dollars can take care of themselves.

WHITE BREADS

		PRICE	DAY
1.	Homemade	22	daily
2.	Buttercrust	24	daily
3.	Cornmeal	26	M F
4.	Dutch Crust	29	W F
5.	French	28	M ThFS
6.	Poppyseed	28	M W
7.	Potato	26	W S
8.	Vienna	26	W T
9.		26	T Th
10.			

SPECIALTY BREADS

1.	Boston Brown	20	M Th
2.	Cinnamon	35	W
3.	Dark Rye	25	W
4.	Egg Twist	30	Th
5.	Garlic Loaf	15	S
6.	Low Sodium	29	T
7.	Raisin	35	MTThS
8.	Oatmeal	28	W
9.	Rye	25	MTThFS
10.	Salt Rising	29	Th
11.	Whole Wheat	32	T S
12.			

DINNER ROLLS

1.	Buns		
2.	Butterbits	40	daily
3.	Butter Crescents	48	daily
4.	Clover	72	F S
5.	Coney Islands	40	MThS
6.	Hard Rolls	40	daily
7.	Hearth Crescents	48	daily
8.	Napkin	15	daily
9.	Parkerhouse	40	W F
10.	Poppyseed	40	daily
11.	Rye Sticks	48	T F S
12.	Baking Powder Biscuits	48	S
13.	Brown n' Serve	40	Seasonal
		48	Seasonal

DONUTS

1.	Apple n spice		
2.	Old Fashion Cake	66	M F S
3.	Fried Cin. Stick	66	W F
4.	Jelly-filled	66	M T
5.	Custard-filled	78	daily
6.	Glazed	78	daily
7.	Honey Cruellers	66	daily
8.	Virginia Reels	66	T Th S
9.		72	W Th S
10.			

COOKIES

SWEET ROLLS

		PRICE	DAY
1.	Bunker Hill		
2.	Coconut	60	M S
3.	Orange Tiffin	50	F
4.	Pan Cinnamon	60	W
5.	Raisin	49	S
6.	Struessel	50	MTWThF
7.	Twist	50	T Th
8.	Chop Suey	50	M W
9.	Caramel Fruit Bun	84	F S
10.		60	S
11.			

DANISH ROLLS

1.	Cinnamon Crisp		
2.	Gems	72	W S
3.	Pecan	50	T S
4.	Princess- each	75	daily
5.	Plain & Jelly	12	W F
6.	Radio	70	daily
7.		75	M Th
8.			

DANISH COFFEE CAKE

1.	Breakfast Stink		
2.	Butter Horn	59	S
3.	Pecan Ring	40	W F
4.	Plain Ring-small	75	MTThFS
5.	Plain Ring-large	35	MTThF
6.		50	S
7.			

COFFEE CAKES

1.	Alligator- small		
2.	Alligator- large	50	daily
3.	Apple-Butterscotch	70	F S
4.	Butter Cinnamon	69	S
5.	Butter- large	40	S
6.	Old Fashion Cheese Cake	60	S
7.	French Custard Ch. Cake	65	W S
8.	Cinnamon Struessel-sm.	65	F
9.	Cinnamon Struessel-lg.	40	MTWFS
10.	Coconut - small	60	S
11.	Dbl Butter- small	40	T S
12.	Dbl Butter- large	40	MThF
13.	Filled Bunt	60	S
14.	Fruit Coffee Cake	49	S
15.	Honey Bee	69	daily
16.	Hungarian	65	W F
17.	Chop Suey	50	MThFS
18.		65	S
19.			

Prices from the good old days are the only bakery items that look more and more attractive with age.

Sometimes the really great headlines just come to us. In the case of "Fresh Cut Trees," it came from one of our designers who called us with the idea while she was driving on vacation—just a day before the presentation.

Party Freshener.

Busken

A Baker Is Always Working

Joe Sr. and his wife, Daisie, needed a vacation in 1956. He hadn't had one for thirty years, if ever. So the hard-working baker and his supportive wife packed their bags—shoot, they probably had to buy bags to pack since a vacation in this family was as rare as a raisin in a winery—and headed off to Europe to take in the sights and sounds of the world's finest cities.

It would also end up being a whirlwind tour of—what else?—bakeries. Joe had the notion that a taste of Europe might sell well in Hyde Park, and upon his return to Cincinnati, tea cookies soon lost display space to petit fours. A new era of sweets had come to the Queen City.

Get a little fresh this year.

Busken

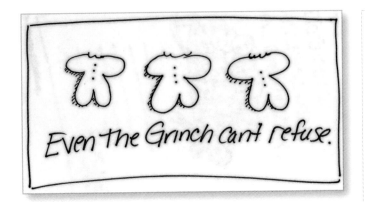

Even the Grinch can't refuse.

Great At Holiday Parties.

Busken

Stress Relief
For The Holidays.

Busken

For maximum appetite appeal, we normally show the Busken product whole and ready to eat. But the Ginger Bread Man was so much more engaging when we broke the rules.

Need A Hand With Your Holiday Baking?

Busken

Keeps getting butter and butter.

Mmmm. Brown n' Serve dinner rolls fresh from the original Virginia Bakery recipe. **Busken**

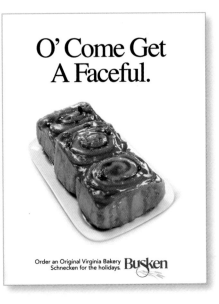

O' Come Get A Faceful.

Order an Original Virginia Bakery Schnecken for the holidays. **Busken**

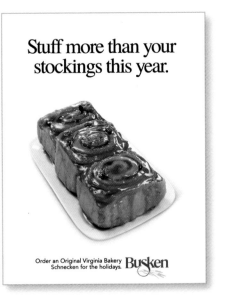

Stuff more than your stockings this year.

Order an Original Virginia Bakery Schnecken for the holidays. **Busken**

Not long after the Virginia Bakery closed, Page Busken hooked up with the former owner, Tom Thie, and struck a deal to keep some of their classic recipes alive in Cincinnati. The delicious result proved for all time that you can mix business with pleasure. The photos were shot in glorious Cinnamonvision by Mark Alexander.

~ The Original Recipe Schnecken ~

Virginia Bakery

NOW AVAILABLE ONLY FROM BUSKEN

Look what
the yuletide
washed in.

Schnecken Keeps Cincinnati Sane

The list of things the average Cincinnatian will line up to buy is long: Reds Opening Day tickets, Jimmy Buffett tickets, an autograph from a Cincinnati Bengal. It's so short it might not even be a list. At least one food item qualifies—the swirling and gooey mass of butter, flour, butter, sugar, butter, cinnamon (and did we mention butter?) known as Schnecken.

Schtock up on Schnecken.

Virginia Bakery Style. **Busken**

When the Thie family owned Virginia Bakery in Clifton, they sold Schnecken only a few times a year and only in earnest on a handful of Saturday mornings leading up to Christmas. Lines formed early in the bitter cold and snow of those holiday mornings. Before daybreak, usually, fans of the pastry came from all over the region clad in goose down and wool to buy the limit of six loaves per person. While waiting for the store to open, they chatted and reminisced about simpler days and laughed about the looniness of waiting two hours or more in the cold for a chance to revisit a childhood treat from another time. Virginia Bakery eventually closed its doors, and the Schnecken tradition in Cincinnati looked like it *was* lost—and for a time it was lost—

until Busken Bakery stepped in to keep it alive.

They had the recipe, but with Schnecken, a recipe is all but meaningless. It's not about what goes into the treat but how the dough is shaped, rested, and kneaded. It took three bakers three months working side by side with Tom Thie of Virginia Bakery before they could get the Schnecken just right. When the Schnecken were ready, Cincinnatians responded. Schnecken flew out the doors. From November 1 to Christmas Eve, the bakery sold an average of twelve Schnecken an hour—that's one every five minutes—every hour, every day and night, every week all the way up until Christmas. It's said that people who try a slab of Schnecken once must have another. Judging by those first-year sales, that's no exaggeration.

Everything
they're crackered
up to be.

Our classic homemade soups are back. Busken

Soup du your.

Our classic homemade soups are back. Busken

Veg Out.

Celebrate
the invention of
the spoon.

Our classic homemade soups are back. Busken

Feels like summer
inside your mouth.

Our classic homemade soups are back. Busken

It's a violation of our creative code to use an exclamation point at the end of a headline. It looks too much like we're overselling. And Busken products sell themselves. "Souprise" was our first exception to this rule in ten years—it just worked better!

All the creatures were stirring.

Our famous soups are back – hot, hearty and prepared fresh each day by hand. Ask for your favorite. **Busken**

Cream of Broccoli. Chicken & Rice. Vegetable. Clam Chowder.

Souprise!

Our classic homemade soups are back. **Busken**

It's beginning to taste a lot like Christmas.
Busken

O' Holey Night.
Busken

Comfort and Joy.
Busken

The bow proved to be a simple way to dress our classic donut for Christmas. And get even more mileage out of the photography.

Who needs a square meal?

Donut look fun?

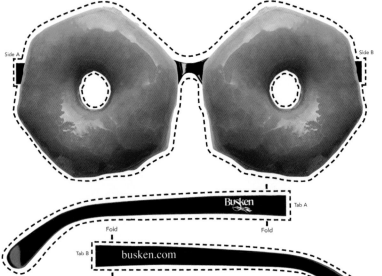

Side A

Side B

Busken

Tab A

Fold

Fold

Tab B

busken.com

Step 1. Print out and cut along dotted lines.

Step 2. Fold where indicated.

Step 3. Apply Tabs A&B to their respective sides with a small amount of tape. Apply liberal amounts of tape to the nose bridge if you own a pocket protector.

Step 4. Put on the Donut glasses and walk around your home, school or office shouting "Hey look, I've got that glazed look in my eyes. Get it? Get it?"

Step 5. Laugh hysterically.

Step 6. The next day, go to Busken and buy a dozen donuts as a peace offering to family, friends and/or co-workers for making a fresh-baked spectacle of yourself.

Step 7. Repeat.

Stop by your neighborhood Busken for real donuts.
Or busken.com for more pretend donuts.

Busken

The "Glazed Look" billboard was one of our earliest efforts at playing with our food in Busken advertising. Later it evolved into the downloadable "Donut Glasses" on the Website.

You've got that glazed look
in your eyes. Busken

Office Supplies.

This morning's special.

Busken

The Busken blend coffee has always been a classic original. It's the daily fuel of Cincinnati business.

Office Supplies.

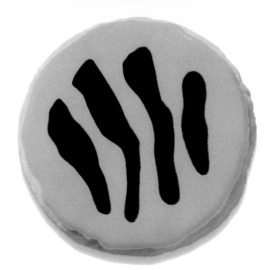

Busken cookie poll to reveal favored stadium site

Busken Bakery will again try to settle, once and for all, the question "Where do the people of Cincinnati really want the Reds stadium?"

Using the bakery's time-honored, cookie poll, voters (and cookie-lovers) may cast their votes by choosing a cookie with either a wedge site design or Broadway Commons logo. A daily tally will be taken by the 13 participating bakeries, two of them downtown. The poll will continue through Saturday, May 2.

Busken has been polling Super Bowl fans for the past 13 years, and has been wrong only twice—once when the Bengals lost to the 49ers

Most recently, the Cincinnati Zoo asked the bakery to run a Baby Elephant poll, in which Cincinnatians were correct in predicting a boy.

Voting by Pocketbook

Tens of thousands of Greater Cincinnatians voted in the first ever Busken Bakery Cookie Poll in 1989—a tally that was a foregone conclusion even before it began in that bitter month of January. The town's beloved Bengals were headed to Super Bowl XXIII. Busken Bakery had enjoyed strong sales of the Icky Sticky bun leading up to the game, and since the 49ers Turnover and Tiger Tail donut sold well, too, why not try a cookie poll?

It was a silly little gesture, but boy oh boy did Cincinnati respond. Cookies flew out the door as revenues flew into the till. In the end, about sixty thousand cookie eaters sided with the Bengals, though a remarkable fifteen hundred holdouts voted with a 49ers cookie, and Cincinnati had a new way to gauge public sentiment.

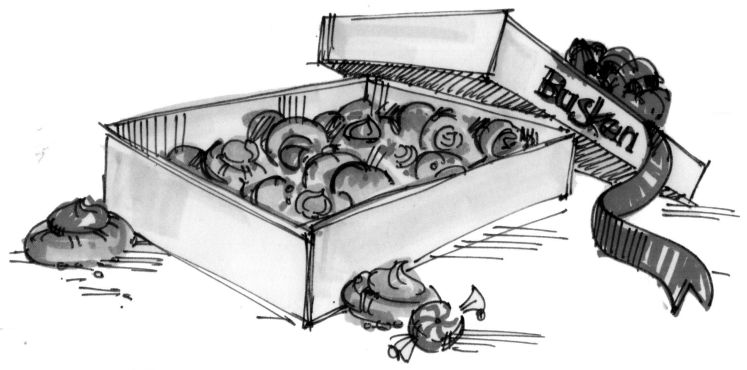

A Truck Full of Goodies & A Big Old Frying Pan

They were called Bob Tailors by the baker who helped them load their trucks and sold sweets to them at wholesale prices. They came to the first Busken Bakery in the back of Hubert's Meat Market in East Hyde Park at daybreak on most mornings, and after exchanging pleasantries and maybe some commentary (When are the Reds gonna get some pitching?) the men filled their panel trucks with bread, muffins, cookies, cream horns, and coffeecakes and headed into the city. It was 1930, and the Great Depression was upon the country. If housewives couldn't get to the bakery, then the bakery would come to them.

Twill Hawkins worked a route in Pleasant Ridge, Hyde Park, and Mount Lookout and had his own way of letting folks know he had arrived on their street. He'd pull onto a block, park his truck, grab a skillet that hung by the door, and clang it until the housewives emerged, babies in arms and quarters in hand. Two donuts for a nickel back then. The heavenly smells were still free.

Remember the pending Y2K disaster when computers had to make the leap from 1999 to 2000? Yeah? Well, neither do we.

Y2Kakes
Still Here.

Busken

Under the Milky Way Tonight

From Sayler Park to Madisonville, Maineville to Price Hill, Anderson Township to Norwood, Cincinnati sleeps at 2 a.m. on a weekday—everywhere but at Busken Bakery in Hyde Park, where the wee hours are prime baking time. Behind a showcase that holds a staggering variety of pastries, one man, baker Charlie Koger, gets ready for work. He dons an apron and tugs on a hair net that looks like a face under a soft peak of meringue. Then he heads through the echoing bakery to a bank of Roto 2000 G Dahlen ovens from Sweden.

Koger needs no manual, no action plan, and no recipe as he moves from one dark oven to the next, poking at digital timers and temperature controls along the way. Behind him are the cakes to bake, a sea of them filling the vast shop. As Koger punches in temperatures and times, each oven responds with a soft sign of heat and chain-driven motion. Koger begins to smooth the batter on top of each cake with a long aluminum spatula. Soon they'll go into the ovens. Another day has dawned in Cincinnati.

CIRCA 1980s

A Sports Car and a Driven Man

In the end, it was all about fifth gear. Old Joe was in semiretirement in 1965, even though he always showed up at his beloved bakery on Saturday mornings before four a.m. to make sure the cakes, muffins, donuts, and Danish were coming off the line without a hitch. He no longer drove a Ford or Chevy, though. The Mercedes he had bought to drive to Saturday-night repasts at Terrace Park Country Club, well, that was in the garage. These mornings Old Joe piloted a Porsche 911, a strange symbol of success for an unassuming man who looked more like a character from a Washington Irving short story than Steve McQueen. Whisper-thin Joe loved the drive to town in his Porsche and would slip seamlessly through the gears on a swift but safe pace down the winding knolls of Indian Hill to Madison Road and finally to his pride-and-joy bakery.

The trip took less than twenty minutes, but it was always something of an unfulfilling jaunt. Why? There was no straight-away long enough to let him get the car into fifth gear. Put a Porsche 911 into fifth gear before its time, and the engine lags in despair.

But Joe realized he could take a different way to work: head east down to still-snoozing Terrace Park, turn back west, and mind the speed limit through town to the flat stretch of highway between Terrace Park and Mariemont. It was the middle of the night, and dawn was still hours away as Joe headed west out of Terrace Park. He knew the bread would be coming out of the ovens and that his bakery would smell great. It would be full of clattering trays and men dressed in baker's whites, their fingers working through the fresh Danish dough.

As the Porsche blew down the deserted four-lane, its headlights clawing through the mist of the Little Miami River, the realization finally came to Joe Busken:

He may have been just a baker, but the company he'd created and built for nearly fifty years was healthy and strong. He knew that both the bakery and this car were overt symbols of success and might spur a little jealousy among some, but he didn't care about that. He never much cared about what anybody thought of his bakery craft or his jaunty baker's cap, and he sure didn't care what anybody thought of his fancy little car. He had worked hard his whole life and deserved this little luxury. Who would begrudge him that? Just outside of town Joe backed off on the gas, hit the clutch and shifted one last time.

He smiled. Finally, fifth gear.

In baking as in life, every crumby ending is a fresh beginning. See you tomorrow.

THE END

Oh wait, look what else we found in the
back of the file cabinet.

GINGERBREAD CAKE

1 c	Ground sugar	Mix butter and sugar until smooth.
¼ c	Butter	
1 c	Molasses	Add molasses and water; mix well.
1½ c	Water	
4 c	All purpose flour	Sift or blend flour, baking soda, ginger, spice, salt, and mix well. Add to above and mix until smooth. Do not over mix.
1 Tbl	Baking soda	
1 Tbl	Ground ginger	
1½ tsp	All spice	
2 tsp	Salt	

Special Instructions: Divide batter into two greased 8-inch square pans.

Baking Temperature: 350° for about 35 minutes until toothpick comes out clean.

CRUNCHY COUNTRY COOKIES

1 c	Butter	Cream the butter and sugar together in a large mixing bowl until it is fluffy and light.
2 c	Light brown sugar	
1	Whole egg	Add one whole egg and mix well.
1 c	Salad oil (Canola if available)	Add the oil and mix well.
1 c	Old fashioned oatmeal	Add nuts, oats, and cornflakes and mix well.
1 c	Cornflakes (crushed)	
½ c	Shredded coconut (recommended)	
½ c	Pecans/Walnuts	
½ c	Whole wheat flour	Add flour, salt, baking soda, and vanilla; mix well.
3 c	Sifted all purpose flour	
1 tsp	Salt	
1 tsp	Baking soda	
1 tsp	Vanilla	

Special Instructions: Form the cookie dough into balls a little smaller than a golf ball. Place on an ungreased cookie sheet. Put a little water on your palm and flatten each ball with your hand.

Baking Temperature: 350° for about 12 minutes. Allow to cool for 10 minutes. Depending on the size of the cookies, you should get about 6-8 dozen.

HOMESTEAD CAKE

1½ c	Sugar	Stew prunes with enough water to
1 c	Cooked prunes	cover. Bring to boil, simmer 10 min.,
		let cool, and drain.
		Mix sugar and prunes until smooth.

¾ c	Water	Mix water, oil, eggs, and vanilla
1 c	Oil	together. Add ½ mixture to above
4	Eggs	and mix until smooth.
1 tsp	Vanilla	

2 c	All purpose flour	Sift flour, cinnamon, nutmeg, salt, and
1 tsp	Cinnamon	baking soda together twice. Add to
1 tsp	Nutmeg	above and mix until smooth. Add the
1 tsp	Salt	rest of the water, oil, eggs, and vanilla
1½ tsp	Baking soda	mixture and mix until smooth.

½ c	Chopped pecans/walnuts	Add chopped nuts and mix.

Baking Temperature: 360° for about 30–35 minutes

HOMESTEAD CAKE TOPPING

¼ lb	Butter	Warm butter and buttermilk to
1 c	Buttermilk	about 140°; do not boil.

1 c	Sugar	
1 Tbl	Honey	Mix all ingredients together.
¼ tsp	Baking soda	

Special Instructions: Make multiple holes in the cake
with a fork. Pour 1 cup of warm topping over cake.
Leave cake in pan to absorb the topping.

MOUNTAIN COOKIES

2½ Tbl	Honey	Mix honey, sugars, butter, salt, and baking soda
1½ c	Ground sugar	until smooth.
1½ c	Brown sugar	
1¼ c	Butter	
1 tsp	Salt	
1 tsp	Baking soda	

2	Large eggs	Soak raisins for 10 min in
1¾ c	Rolled oats	warm water, and drain.
2½ c	All purpose flour	Add eggs, oats, flour, raisins,
2 c	Raisins (soaked and drained)	nuts, and chocolate chips
3 c	Chopped English walnuts	to above and gently mix to
2 c	Chocolate chips	incorporate.

Special Instructions: Scoop dough (golf ball size) with spoon or ice
cream scoop on greased cookie sheet. Space cookies out to allow for
spreading during baking. Careful to not over bake.

Baking Temperature: 350° for about 12 to 14 min.

The Creative Dept. and Busken Bakery (Lauren Anderson, Page Busken, Brian Busken, Dan Busken, and Steve Deiters) toast the success of their biggest ad effort to date—cookies for giant people. Busken truck photo courtesy of Mark Alexander (Alexander + Associates).

Acknowledgements.

Busken Bakery would like to thank the following individuals for their contributions during the creation of this crumby book: Joe Busken Jr., Linda Busken Jergens, John Eckberg, Page and Lucille Busken, Christian Busken, Brian Busken, Dan Busken, Sarah Busken-Frisdma, Shawn Busken, Stephen Busken, the Chip and Susan Hunter family, Steve Deiters, Lauren Anderson, Dave Fagin, Michael Comstock, Troy Hitch, Laura Moser, and the many talented creatives who have helped craft the identity that the bakery enjoys today. We also thank the entire staff of bakers, decorators, finishers, maintenance and sanitation workers, drivers, office staff, and retail clerks at Busken Bakery. Thanks, too, to Richard Hunt, Jack Heffron, Howard Cohen and all those behind the scenes at Clerisy Press. We also want to thank David Lindner at the United Dairy Farmers for introducing us to The Creative Department ten years ago. Also thanks to our photographers: Teri Campbell (Teri Studios), Mark Alexander (Alexander + Associates), Greg Kuchik (Kuchik Photography). We can't forget our friends Chuck Martin and Polly Campbell at the Cincinnati Enquirer, The Tom Norton Family of Norton Outdoor Advertising, Dan Monk at the Cincinnati Business Courier and The Ralph Blackwelder Jr. Family. And, finally, a special thanks to Bill Remke, Eric Rabe, and Don Fine of Remke Markets, for helping make the Busken name a household word in Northern Kentucky.

Founded in 1992 by Lauren Anderson and Steve Deiters, the Creative Department is an ad agency that has built its business by breathing life into brands and framing communications in delightfully compelling ways—whether traditional, interactive or guerilla. Their rebel band of 19 (and counting) highly creative individuals includes creative directors, writers, art directors, production artists, project managers, designers, brand strategists, interactive marketers and developers. Their nationally award-winning work has been featured in publications around the world. And locally, their long-running advertising campaign for Busken Bakery has grown to become legendary (at least in their minds).

John Eckberg grew up in Manchester, Ohio, where he developed a taste for pastries while stocking shelves and cleaning butcher blocks at Mike's Meat Market. He attended Akron University, graduated from Ohio University and has been a journalist at the *Cincinnati Enquirer* since 1980. His work has been published in the *New York Times, Newsweek, USA Today* and many other national print and Web publications. The author of *The Success Effect: Uncommon Conversations with America's Business Trailblazers* and the true crime thriller *Road Dog,* Eckberg is also fond of Schnecken and has been known to wait in line for hours on bitter cold December mornings with pal Jack Roehr to buy his limit of six loaves.

The Donut Heads of Busken Bakery (as seen on busken.com) are already generating sweet plans for next year. Stay tuned, Cincinnati.